Made in the USA
Middletown, DE
01 May 2021

38794311R00070